From Cinnabar
to Quicksilver

J. Howard Campbell

New Almaden Quicksilver County Park
Association wishes to acknowledge the efforts
of its members, especially Art Boudreault, who
edited the copy, and Bruce Bartlett, who was
responsible for the book and cover designs.
Lyle Bartlett also provided significant editing
review.

ISBN 978-0-578-01486-9

Published by   New Almaden Quicksilver County Park Association
              P.O Box 124
              New Almaden, California, 95042

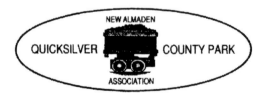

This book is dedicated to Kitty Monahan, for
her hard work and enthusiasm to keep the New
Almaden Quicksilver Mine program alive and
succeeding nicely.

Jim Campbell
Author
Artist

Preface

At the southern edge of San Jose, California, lies the little community of New Almaden, once a bustling, gritty mining area known as The Hacienda. In the hills above New Almaden is the 4,200-acre Almaden Quicksilver County Park, home to wildlife, wildflowers, miles of hiking trails, and the occasional reminder that this was once the largest and richest mine in all of California and home to two communities known as Spanishtown and Englishtown. For more than one hundred years here, miners dug out chunks of a red rock called cinnabar, which, when roasted and distilled, releases its treasure, quicksilver, also known as mercury.

Long before the miners arrived, the native Indians of the Santa Clara valley first used a red mineral they called *mohetka* by pounding it into a powder and mixing it with tallow, which they used as a paint to decorate their bodies. In 1845, nearly three years before the discovery of gold in California, the first quicksilver mine in the state came into existence. The New Almaden Mine produced upwards of $70,000,000 worth of quicksilver, the greatest amount produced by any individual mine in California.

Until 1865, the Almaden mines of Spain were the world's largest producers of quicksilver. That year, New Almaden exceeded the production of the Spanish mines and equaled them for the following thirty years.

Today very little remains of the New Almaden Mining Company, the world's largest quicksilver mining company. The miners are gone, but their legacy remains in the many homes along Almaden Road and in the Casa Grande, former home of the mine managers and now home to a museum filled with artifacts and memories of a time gone by.

The town of New Almaden is located south of San Jose, off the Almaden Expressway. The Museum is located at 21350 Almaden Rd. and is open Friday, Saturday, and Sunday, except for major holidays. The museum exhibits the collection of Constance Perham, showing blacksmith workings, the history of mercury mining, and the lifestyles of mining communities at New Almaden. There is no fee for admission, and a walking tour is available. Please call 408-323-1107 for further information, or to arrange a special group or school tour. The Almaden Quicksilver county park, open from 8:00am to sunset, encompasses the mining landscape and several historic buildings.

Contents

About the Author and Artist

J. Howard (Jim) Campbell was born in Detroit, Michigan, in 1928. As a young man he worked for his father in a small-town newspaper and printing office in Ansonia, Ohio. It was here that he learned his life-long profession in the printing and newspaper field. In 1948, he married Joanne Dohse, and from Ohio they moved to San Jose, California.

In 1975, Jim formed his own company reproducing his original art into prints that can be found in prestigious galleries, maritime museums, and shops around the country. Many of his drawings have won awards in competitive art shows.

Thirty of Jim's pen-and-ink drawings of historic California landmarks have been commissioned for use by the United States Postal Service in forms of commemorative cancellations and cachet designs, bringing mini-reproductions of the artist's work to stamp collectors throughout the country.

Campbell's art work now hangs in private collections throughout the world in Japan, Hong Kong, Germany, England, Canada, and the United States.

Certificate for 100 Shares of Stock

The certificate on the following page is for 100 shares of stock in the Quicksilver Mining Company. The date on this certificate is 1866. On the left side, notice a mercury barometer, and on the right side a mercury thermometer.

The Best Kept Secret of Santa Clara County

Did you know that

• The first mining claim in California was made in San Jose?

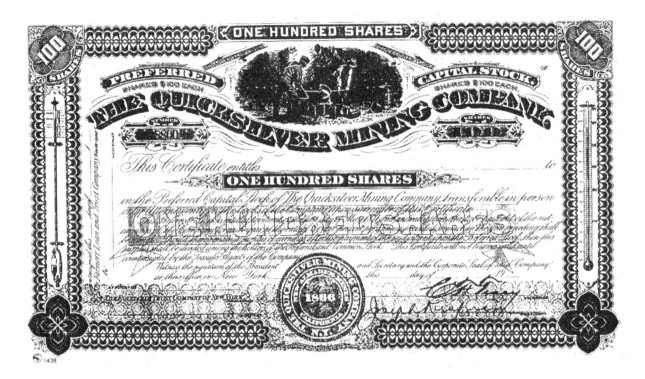

- Quicksilver (mercury) was discovered 27 months before gold was discovered in California? The discovery was made in November 1845.

- The second largest quicksilver mine in the world was located in New Almaden, California?

- From 1845 to 1976, seven New Almaden mines produced nearly 84 million pounds of quicksilver?

- The mines still contain cinnabar, the ore from which quicksilver comes?

- Mercury contamination makes it unsafe to eat any fish caught in the Guadalupe Reservoir at the Almaden Quicksilver County Park?

- Quicksilver was the world's chief reduction agent of gold and silver?

- Until the discovery of the New Almaden mine in California, the English banking house of Rothschild owned and operated the Almaden Mercury Mines in Almaden, Spain?

- The New Almaden Mines saved California's Mother Lode, Nevada's Comstock Lode and gold and silver mines in America from domination by foreign capital?

- During the Civil War California nearly went to the Confederacy? A group of New York financiers took advantage of Lincoln and tried to use him to take over the mines and the West.

- The only quicksilver mine museum in the United States is in New Almaden, California?

From Cinnabar to Quicksilver

The Ohlone Indians knew of the vermilion red rock, cinnabar, which they obtained from a secret cave in the nearby hills. Today the location of that cave is part of the Almaden Quicksilver County Park. The Indians crushed this red rock into a powder and used it for face paint. The original Mission in Santa Clara, which no longer exists, had its walls painted with this red paint.

The first non-natives to be attracted to the vivid red rock were Antonio Sunol and Luis Chaboya, in 1824. They attempted to extract silver from the rock, but their efforts were fruitless.

During the fall of 1845, Andres Castillero, a captain in the military service of Mexico, arrived at Mission Santa Clara and while there he observed the reddish color applied to the walls of the Mission. He also was interested in the small quantity of red rock piled in the courtyard. Castillero had to resume his duties and it was not until much later that he was able to return to the Mission and discuss the topic of red rock with Father del Real. Castillero was able to find the source of the red rock with the help of local Indians about fifteen miles from the Mission.

Convinced that the rock was significant and possibly might contain gold or silver, Castillero vigorously proceeded to break up pieces of the rock. This material reminded him of a similar type of rock he had seen in his native country, Spain. The quicksilver mines of La Mancha, one of the world's greatest mines, had been mining cinnabar-producing mercury for centuries. He was sure that the material he was dealing with was similar.

Castillero experimented by roasting some of the rock over a continuous fire. He was elated to discover small globular particles of a silvery nature, which proved to him that the roasted rock was quicksilver, another name for mercury.

On November 22, 1845, Castillero made the necessary preparations for filing a statement of declaration and went to the office of Pedro Chabolla, the Alcalde in Pueblo San Jose. It might be noted that this became the first mine of any kind in California; the gold rush would not come along until 1848. Castillero performed what he considered the necessary steps to file his claim, but to make doubly certain, when he returned to Mexico City, he petitioned the government to further validate his title.

Meanwhile, the United States occupied California, and Castillero had failed to achieve any success. With the obligation of military service, he decided to sell his shares in the Santa Clara Mine to the Barron, Forbes Company, located in Tepic, Mexico. They became the first industrial operators of the mine.

The story of Andres Castillero came to an abrupt ending in 1847. His identity, as the discoverer of quicksilver and the first legal mining claim in California, would become lost in the pages of history. Castillero vanished into obscurity, not knowing that his discovery would soon obtain worldwide prominence as one of the greatest quicksilver mines.

Before the first drops of the liquid quicksilver were extracted from the roasted ore, the Santa Clara Mine became the New Almaden Mines. Under Barron, Forbes operation, the mines yielded more than one-third of all quicksilver produced in the United States. The quicksilver was deposited in vats and from there it was ladled to the scales where its weight was accurately measured and poured into iron flasks. The flasks were 18 inches in length, 8 inches in diameter and ¼ inch thick. Each flask contained 76 pounds of quicksilver. With their wagons loaded with flasks, teamsters left the Hacienda at regular intervals for the little village seaport of Alviso.

The port of Alviso from 1850 through 1863 played an important role as terminal point for freight and passenger service in the South Bay. Peter Burnett, the first governor, had his home built here, thinking that someday Alviso would be a major port and city. However, that failed to materialize, and Burnett had his house dismantled and rebuilt in San Jose.

The first steamer to travel between Alviso and San Francisco was the converted scow, the *Sacramento*. Passengers were charged $40 for a one-way ticket. A stage service carried passengers from the boat on a course through Santa Clara to San Jose for a $5.00 fare.

The discovery of gold in 1848 by James Marshall on the American River at Coloma changed California forever. California gold and Nevada silver, both dependent upon quicksilver for amalgamation, shared in this economic blessing.

The mine hill at New Almaden was like a gopher colony with a maze of more than 100 miles of tunnels and 21 shafts, many over a thousand feet deep. One shaft was bottomed on the 2450-foot level, 750 feet below sea level. The underground works in area was roughly two miles square and a half-mile deep.

One of the longer legal contests in US history concerned land claims centered on the New Almaden Mines. However, the mines continued to operate during this period. The Barron, Forbes Company sold its interest in New Almaden to the Quicksilver Mining Company in 1863. Their short span of 13 years was highly successful. With a minimum investment they would produce quicksilver valued at $15,000,000. They pioneered a company that would continue to flourish for a half-century and established a settlement still known as New Almaden.

In 1863, Samuel Butterworth arrived in New Almaden to become General Manager in complete charge of operations. His rules and regulations were imposed on the employees. Only qualified and competent workers were retained on the payroll. Butterworth's management had grossed for the company $1,950,345. The largest number of employees ever to work at New Almaden was engaged at this time, with 1,112 persons on the payroll.

The influence of the Barron, Forbes days was diminishing. Under Butterworth the company proclaimed itself a private industrial institution. The mining area was posted as private property and fenced in to control all of the traffic of peddlers or trespassers. A tollgate was established at the entrance to the property and outsiders were admitted only with official approval. The most important innovation initiated by Butterworth was the tramway system on the slopes, which descended from the mine areas in Englishtown and Spanishtown to the furnaces below at the Hacienda.

In 1867, the mine included villages with over 700 buildings, most of which were dwellings. At the mine was a population of 1,800 souls and at the Hacienda were about 600 more. The total number of men working for the company was about 1,000.

The average duration of the life of men who worked underground was 45 years. Arsenic and sulfate in the mercury was always a problem. The men worked one day a week at the furnaces, then changed to do something else. The men worked 10 to 12-hour shifts, six days a week. This was also a time when steam engines were in use. These engines were located at the hoisting works, and were powerful enough to lift a load from 2,400 feet below the surface, or about 700 feet below sea level.

The career of Samuel Butterworth came to an end in 1870. James Randol became the new General Manager. Randol established residence in the Casa Grande. He made changes at the mine and brought in new furnaces that used less fuel and maintained a consistent temperature, with no cooling off period. The new furnaces operated day and night.

James Randol greatly improved conditions at the mines. Now the mines operated with two work shifts. The miners worked underground from 7:00 to 5:00 p.m. with one hour for lunch. On Sundays and holidays, the work stopped in the mines and on the surface, except at the furnaces.

The James B. Randol shaft, on a spur of Mine Hill, continued as a great producer until 1896. The Randol produced over $10,000,000 in quicksilver during its years of operation. It terminated at the 1,800-foot level. The Santa Isabel shaft was started in 1877 and reached a depth of 2,300 feet. It was the deepest shaft extended from the ground surface. In the deep laterals, mules were used for tramming and were stabled underground.

In the days prior to Randol, payday was an alarming event; the "ladies of the night" came from San Jose along with professional gamblers. Whiskey and wine flowed freely, and it was not unusual to have at least one knifing or a murder. New Almaden had become a retreat for cutthroats, gamblers, and all sorts of thieves.

The regime of James Randol brought the mines to their most productive and profitable years. He helped to improve the miners' dwellings; the company maintained the homes with necessary repairs. The houses were enclosed with picket fences. Plants and shrubs were also furnished. A monthly rental fee of about $5.00 was paid to the mining company. In 1871, Randol, conferring with many of the employees, conceived and organized a health and welfare plan that provided medical service for the employees and their families. He promoted recreation activities, and in 1885 the company assumed the cost of two buildings, one in Englishtown and the other in the Hacienda.

These buildings became known as the Helping Hands Clubs. These clubs supplied a place of amusement and meeting halls for the miners' families independent of the drinking saloon. The company kept three public schools and two churches in repair. A Miners' Fund was established to benefit all the workers and their families.

When the New Almaden Mines became a major institution in 1850, more than 500 workers were sent here from Mexico and other Hispanic American countries. Spanishtown became a community of 2,500 people. This settlement was located on a spur connecting Mine and Graveyard Hills. The Cornish miners came from Cornwall, England in the 1860s. They settled on the east flank of Mine Hill in what became known as Englishtown. Everything was company owned and operated. The Mexican and Cornish miners were some of the best hard rock miners in California.

The Cornish miners were well known for their physical attributes for this rigorous work, and their hard-rock mining skills made them among the best for efficiency and endurance. A Cornish man would be referred to as "Cousin Jack" all through the mining communities. What is now known as New Almaden was the Hacienda, where the furnace workers lived.

A miner by the name of Bertram Barrett lost his arm in a mining accident and his arm was buried in the Hacienda cemetery, but the rest of his body was buried in the Oak Hill Cemetery in San Jose. Bertram was quite a card player and could shuffle cards with one hand better than most men in two hands. It was something else to see him tie his shoes with one hand.

New Almaden had produced upward of $70,000,000 in quicksilver. Any California mine that seems to have exceeded this production figure had done so not as an individual mine, but as a combination of mines.

During the Civil War, a group of New York financiers took advantage of President Lincoln's preoccupation with government affairs and tried to use him to gain possession of the mine. Fortunately an 11th hour telegram was received and informed the President of the true nature of things. If President Lincoln had used military force to seize the mine for these financiers, every mining title in California and Nevada would have been upset, and these states would have certainly deserted the Union to join the Confederacy.

Today very little remains of the original New Almaden Mining Company, but the memory of its heyday has been kept alive by local leaders.

The New Almaden Mines are the most documented mine in California. Thanks to Robert Bulmore, amateur photographer and the General Agent for the company, for the many photographs taken between 1889 and 1912. He held this position until December 1899, when the same was abolished due to the decline in quicksilver production. The Bulmore family was the last official occupant of the Casa Grande. And thanks to his son, Laurence Bulmore, who co-authored the book *Cinnabar Hills* and preserved his family's memory.

The Reduction Works of Almaden 1893

This drawing of the Reduction Works at Almaden Mine was made from a glass photographic plate taken about 1880 when the mine was operating at high capacity. The New Almaden was the first workable quicksilver mine in North America. The reduction works, where cinnabar was heated to extract the quicksilver, had Scott furnaces, which subsequently revolutionized the industry. Not pictured in this drawing are the two brick chimney stacks of the old Scott furnaces. They were located on the hill to the right of this picture.

There were furnaces on both sides of Los Alamitos Creek, a large stock of wood, and a rail line to allow the ore carts to travel easily to both sides of the creek. In the foreground, mine officials worked in the mine office buildings. They were among the last remaining buildings to stand. The mine office served as a dwelling occupied by Harry Austin.

Reduction Works, 1976, 16 x 20 in.

The Casa Grande

The Casa Grande showplace of 1854 has faded, but it was once the 27-room home for the 19th century managers of the New Almaden Quicksilver Mines. This grand old historical building is still a gem in Santa Clara County. Today, part of the building houses a mining museum of treasures from the prime days of mining in New Almaden.

The Santa Clara County Parks and Recreation Department plans to restore the 150-year-old, three-level building as it looked in the 1890s when the New Almaden Quicksilver Mine was the largest mining operation in California.

There actually are three sections of The Casa Grande. The oldest section, probably built about 1849, is a single-story structure where most of the mining museum is located today.

In 1852, mine manager Henry Halleck, who became one of the highest-ranking Union Army generals during the Civil War, commissioned the construction of a hotel for visitors and company dignitaries.

When the building was finished in 1854, Halleck named it The Casa Grande (the big house). Halleck never lived there, but instead used the house for entertainment. It was furnished with crystal chandeliers, hand-carved fireplace frames with inlaid mother-of-pearl, thick carpets, and French furniture.

The Casa Grande became the high-society center in New Almaden, with garden parties and musical entertainment to host visiting dignitaries ranging from wealthy mine investors to representatives of the emperor of China.

In the 1880s, J. B. Randol commissioned new grounds on the six-acre site. John McLaren, who later designed San Francisco's Golden Gate Park, landscaped the Casa Grande.

The Mansion was sold in 1926 to the Black Brothers. Two years later they converted the Casa Grande into a swim resort, called Club Almaden. In 1963, new owners converted a ballroom into a theater called the Opry House for old time melodrama acts. Fifteen years later, the Opry House was enlarged, extending the backstage area into the main house's parlor.

In 1973 the county parks department began buying the mine properties and purchased the Casa Grande in 1997. The following year, the present museum, which had been in a house down the street, was moved into the refurbished one-story section of the Casa Grande.

Casa Grande

Campbell

Casa Grande, 1999, 16 x 20 in.

The Hacienda

The Hacienda was the headquarters of the first mine in California, beginning in 1847. The little settlement was built at the base of the hills on the tree-lined stream which was called the Arroyo de las Alamitos (the little river of the poplar trees). Running along the front of the homes was a man-made ditch called the *acequia*, where water from the furnace yard coursed its way through the village and returned to the creek at the outskirts of town. It was a source of water for the cottage gardens along the way. In 1861, the first Post Office was opened with John Brodie as the first Postmaster.

The journey from San Jose to Almaden was twelve miles by horse and buggy. The gateway to the Hacienda began at the Casa Grande and ended at the great furnaces. The road from San Jose was fringed with groves of cottonwood, sycamore, and willow trees. Two lines of stages made a daily trip each way, so passengers from San Francisco could reach the mines within four or five hours.

The general store was the gathering place for miners and furnace employees in the heyday of the Hacienda. Today, the Hacienda is a quiet village with many of the houses of the early furnace men still standing. The acequia is gone and the dirt road has been paved, but portions of the old brick sidewalk remain. The New Almaden store, constructed in 1849, was still in business in 1930. The store was converted into a bar and post office, which flourished until a fire destroyed the original landmark in 1973. In 1874, the Hacienda experienced a fire, which destroyed many of the miners' homes. Soon after, James Randol installed a system of fire hydrants and constructed a bell tower to alert the village and call the bucket brigade to action.

In the 1870s, Thomas Derby acquired the general stores on the hill and in the Hacienda. He introduced the credit system known as "Boletos." The stores carried no credit accounts. As the company advanced no wages before payday, the store would issue small cardboard inscriptions called Boletos. Originally these were brass coins in denomination up to a dollar. A miner without funds, wishing to make a purchase, was issued the desired amount. In these transactions, a record was sent to the company paymaster who deducted the stated amount from the miner's wages. The company encouraged the system because it meant less cash would have to be paid out at the end of the month. There were occasions when miners wanting cash would draw Boletos debited against the payroll.

The General Store, 1988, 16 x 20 in.

Carson Adobe

The Carson Adobe is one of the few remaining company-owned employee houses. It was constructed sometime between 1848 and 1850, probably by Mexican workers brought to work the mines in 1847 by Alexander Forbes. The adobe was made up of three fairly large rooms arranged quite differently from the usual adobes built at this time.

The earliest known occupant whose name is on record is James Brodie, company bookkeeper, and in July 1861 the first postmaster and justice of the peace at New Almaden. In November 1949, Connie Perham, who lived in Carson Adobe at the time, made her dream come true. Connie and two others established the first New Almaden Historical Society. Later she met Doug Perham, a successful electrical engineer and longtime collector of artifacts and Indian memorabilia. They married and devoted their life to developing the New Almaden Museum. This is the only mercury mining museum in the United States. The Perhams are gone now, but their legacy lives on. This was a museum where you didn't just observe. Connie passed around a bottle of ore containing mercury and a bottle without mercury; you could really tell the difference in weight. Today the New Almaden Mining Museum is located in the Casa Grande.

In the 1920s the Hacienda houses were sold off by the successors of the Quicksilver Mining Company, and the town became a village. If you're searching for a Sunday retreat from the sounds of the city, venture to New Almaden.

Carson Adobe, 2005, 16 x 20 in.

A Hacienda Cottage

The charm of the Hacienda is still present in the village of New Almaden. For many years after the Quicksilver Mining Company liquidation, the little town was practically deserted as the miners moved on to new fields of endeavor. However, New Almaden never died as newcomers discovered the original cottages along the tree-shaded thoroughfare. The spirit of New Almaden came back and still prevails today. There are two types of homes, wood homes and adobe brick and plaster, lining both sides of the Almaden Road.

The early residents of the Hacienda received their water from the acequia (the Spanish term for the man-made ditch), which came from the reduction works. The acequia offered water for domestic purposes, for livestock, and for gardens and flowers. The water flowed through the ditch on the east side of the Almaden Road to a point just below the Hacienda School.

Life was quiet in the Hacienda as the greater percentage of the population lived on the hill. The colorful gardens and rambling vines attached to the porch trellis works and the white picket fences out front gave a charm quite unique to this little village. This drawing is a typical cottage as it looked before 1900.

Hacienda Cottage, 2004, 16 x 20 in.

Hacienda Hotel in 1924

This building was originally a boarding house built along the banks of the Alamitos Creek. Later it was converted to a small hotel to accommodate visitors who came to the mining settlement. After the mining operation officially closed in 1912, only a few residences remained in the village of deserted buildings. The boarding house stood vacant for many years until it was remodeled to serve as a restaurant. The old structure with new trim and paint became known as Café Del Rio.

When Karl and Helen Resch first came to New Almaden in the early 1930s there was no public water supply or garbage service in the area. Helen helped to change that and opened her rustic restaurant, which soon became a focal point in town. The restaurant became well known for its Italian dishes, such as *Chicken Almaden*. Helen Resch ran the Café Del Rio with her husband of 37 years until he died in 1971. Mrs. Resch continued to keep the restaurant open until selling it in 1979. Today, the restaurant is called La Forêt, an upscale French dinner house.

Hacienda Hotel 1924   Campbell

Hacienda Hotel, 2004, 16 x 20 in.

Mining ceased in 1976 and all the shafts and tunnels were closed. The Santa Clara Department of Parks and Recreation acquired the entire mining property by 1976, and most of the land has been open for public use since 1975. Within the park, are the historical sites of Englishtown, Spanishtown, and the Hacienda.

In 1985, the County purchased the museum collection of Constance Perham, who for many years displayed mining artifacts, memorabilia and photographs. This private museum was established in 1949 by Mrs. Perham and operated by her until 1983 when she retired. Today the museum is located in the Casa Grande.

With the passing of time, the heyday of this little mining community that covered a half century faded with the gradual passage of its pioneers. In 1964, officials of the U.S. Department of the Interior unveiled a plaque including the village of New Almaden as a national historic landmark.

Helping Hand Club in Hacienda

In 1886, the mine manager, James Randol, initiated the plan to construct a recreational hall in the Hacienda. The building was built by Miles McDougal of San Jose. The Helping Hand Club had a large assembly hall, game and card room, and kitchen. The club also had a stage that was patterned after the Tivoli theater in San Francisco.

A small library containing 450 volumes relating to history, science, fiction, and juvenile literature was used by the miners in their leisure time. Weekly and daily newspapers included the San Francisco Examiner, the San Jose Mercury, the San Jose Times, The Alta, and the London Times.

Every convenience for recreation and leisure time was offered to the workers by the company. Everybody who paid $1 a month to the Miner's Fund was entitled to all privileges for the use of the club. No gambling or drinking was allowed. The building stood for many years following the closing of the mines and was dismantled in 1941.

Music was important to the New Almaden miners. The villagers were entertained at various functions by the colorful costumed brass band. The Mountain Echo Band was organized on the Hill in 1890 and was made up of members from Spanishtown and Englishtown. Though small, the brass band was a delight and very popular in the mining community.

Helping Hand Club, 2004, 20 x 16 in.

The Bulmore House

Robert Bulmore, a native Londoner, served in various capacities in accounting from 1878 to 1899. He was the Hacienda foreman, cashier, and general agent on the Pacific Coast.

New Almaden had a large overseas trade and Bulmore understood its intricacies. He knew how to handle complex problems and was highly respected by the 400 or more men working at the mine. The Bulmore family participated in all community activities and Robert had gained a reputation for amateur theatricals. Bulmore was also a competent photographer. During the industrial zenith of the mine in the 1880s, he and his close friend, Dr. S. Winn, would record the Quicksilver Mining Company history.

It is to Laurence Bulmore, Robert's son, that he owes a great deal. Laurence spent years gathering copies of his father's photos after the negatives had been destroyed. Laurence was one of the three founders of the New Almaden Historical Society. In 1967, along with Milton Lanyon, Bulmore published *Cinnabar Hills*, the story of life and times in New Almaden. The book was dedicated to the miners and their families who lived and worked in Englishtown, Spanishtown, and the Hacienda. Laurence and his wife were a real force in preserving Santa Clara County's history.

Bulmore House, 1988, 16 x 20 in.

The Randol Shaft

The world famous Randol shaft was started in 1871, and by 1874 the Randol was 672 feet deep. The Randol had gone some 700 feet deep before it produced a bonanza of ore. Work in the shaft ran virtually night and day for many years. Every miner on the hill worked in its depths. The cinnabar mined here produced over 275,000 flasks of quicksilver.

The shaft was commenced on a spur of the Mine Hill, and continued as a great provider until 1896. The Randol laterals uncovered ore bodies 100 to 300 feet wide and 12 to 20 feet thick. This mine proved to be abundantly rich and produced over $10,000,000 in quicksilver during its years of operation. The Randol terminated any further development at the 1,800-foot level.

James B. Randol ended his career at the New Almaden mines in 1892, at which time he had concluded twenty-two years as a superb manager of one of the world's great quicksilver mines. The mines attained the peak of their development under Randol's management. These were to be the bonanza years of the New Almaden mines.

When Randol retired, Mr. Robert Bulmore was appointed General Agent and Pacific Coast representative for the company. Bulmore held this position until December 1899, when the job was abolished due to the decline of quicksilver production. The Bulmore family was the last official occupant of the Casa Grande.

James B. Randol Shaft, 1988, 16 x 20 in.

Captain James Harry Shaft

This was an exploratory project started in 1893 and was the last major shaft of the Quicksilver Mining Company. The shaft was named for the man who spent many years as a mining captain in the underground workings of New Almaden mines. The Captain James Harry shaft terminated at a depth of 800 feet.

Robert Bulmore wrote the following at James Harry's death, "His death is deeply regretted by the men who daily risked their lives with him in the bowels of the earth."

California's gold miners, who used mercury in processing the precious metal, avoided importing costs when they found a steady supply of mercury from New Almaden. Some $500,000,000 dollars' worth of mercury was produced in New Almaden before mining ceased in 1975. This represented more cash dollars than those produced by any other single mine in California.

Captain James Harry Shaft, 2003, 16 x 20 in.

Cousin Jack

The settlement of Englishtown was situated on a ridge that was part of the hills called Cuchilla de la Miña (blades of the mine). The inhabitants were from Cornwall, England. As a mining camp, it was unique in many ways; the people were living in an environment much different from the typical mining camps. The camp was greatly influenced by the attitude of the mining company. Saloons, dance halls, ladies of the night, and other features, were inconspicuous.

By 1866, conditions in Cornwall had reached a point of disastrous proportions. The copper mines were becoming fewer in operation and unemployment had increased. Thousands of families faced starvation. During 1866, an estimated 5,000 miners left Cornwall and came to America. They spread themselves from the copper mines in Michigan to the mining camps of the West. Their physical attributes for this rigorous work as hard-rock miners placed them among the best in efficiency and endurance. They were intelligent but in many cases were illiterate, having started their life in the mines at an early age with little formal schooling.

Jack being a common name among the Cornish, it was not long before each new arrival from Cornwall was referred to as "Cousin Jack."

In the background are furnaces 1 and 2 located on the banks of the Alamitos creek. These furnaces designed by H.J. Huttner, engineer, and built by Robert Scott, brick mason, revolutionized the reduction of quicksilver. These furnaces allowed continuous firing, reducing the time to roast a charge of ore from eight days to 28 hours.

"Cousin Jack" New Almaden Mine, 2004, 16 x 20 in.

Buena Vista Pump House

The Buena Vista shaft was designed to handle all the water in the mine. Today, after nearly a hundred years and despite the fact that over fifty years ago all the machinery was dynamited from the foundation, the sandstone and granite blocks are as perfectly fitted as when they were first built. The massive granite block foundation was the most substantial and elaborate of the entire shaft buildings.

The Buena Vista pump engine was the largest ever built and was a mechanical marvel in its day. This power plant had a giant flywheel measuring 24 feet in diameter. When assembled in its granite-lined pit, it could pump eight strokes per minute and brought water up from a depth of 2,300 feet, 600 feet below sea level. Unfortunately, at this level, the Cornish pump could no longer pump the water out as quickly as the water poured in.

Today, there is little water available in the Quicksilver County Park. No one ever pumped or laid pipes to deliver water to the miners' living areas. There are no residents living in the park today. You must carry your own water in with you, just as they did one hundred fifty years ago.

In 1934, the county completed the Almaden reservoir to hold back the water flow of the Los Alamitos and Twin Creeks. When the project was finished, someone carelessly tipped their outhouse over, polluting the Los Alamitos Creek, which was New Almaden's only source of water. Typhoid swept through the community. There were no deaths but many people became sick. A petition circulated demanding a grand jury investigation of the critical water problem. Following the investigation, a hookup with city water was done for the entire New Almaden community.

Buena Vista Pump House, 2003, 16 x 20 in.

The Santa Isabel Shaft

The Santa Isabel shaft was started in 1877 and reached a depth of 2300 feet. It was the deepest shaft extending from the ground surface and during its years of activity, it was an excellent producer. An added feature in this mineshaft was the discovery in 1893 of the first carbon dioxide gas in California.

The mine company found a new use for one of the mine's greatest hazards. Two men named Pfeffer and Meyer hit upon the idea of liquefying carbonic acid gas. They made a deal with the company to bottle it and pay the company ten cents per cylinder. The discovery area was sealed and taken over by Pfeffer and Meyer. They ran a pipe to the dam on the 1,400-foot level and were instantly in business. This was actually the start of the dry ice industry in the United States.

The two men were so successful that they desired to build a plant near the railroad below and extended the pipeline to this point. The Mine Company said, "No" to any plans for this operation. Pfeffer and Meyer told the company what it could do with its gas and the gas is there to this day.

The Santa Isabel, 2004, 16 x 20 in.

The Miners of New Almaden

The New Almaden mine was the largest, richest mine this state has ever known. It produced more metallic wealth than any of the gold mines of 1849. The quicksilver mine played a major role in the gold and silver bonanza that opened the West and brought miners from all over the world.

The miners came from Mexico and Cornwall to work the vast tunnels and shafts that riddled the hills of New Almaden. They worked in perpetual darkness in the underground with ever-present dangers. Immense volumes of carbon dioxide gas, which was odorless, colorless, and heavier than air, and underground water that could flood a shaft were always a fear.

It took a special type of man to work out chunks of rich cinnabar and to load the ore cars. This phase of mining was called "tramming." Workers transported the ore through the tunnels to the shaft where it was hoisted to the surface. After the ore was sorted, wagon teams hauled the ore to the tramway where the cars were loaded for descent to the furnace yard. In the early days, the only light in the underground mines was from candles. In a 24-hour day, 60 pounds of candles were used.

A story often told took place in the last days of the Church Shaft. Two men nearly lost their lives there. They had been lowered to the bottom to release a valve; since the area was flooded with carbon dioxide, this task had to be done instantly. One of the men became so weak that he could not move. The other miner was able to free the valve, and not a second too soon, for the gas had been stirred up and enveloped them both. When they reached the cage, they gave a signal to hoist. On the way up the compact cage got stuck. The gas had reached suffocating proportions; they were boxed in with no possibility of escape. They had resigned themselves that this was the end of the line for them. Then all of a sudden the cage shook in the darkness of the shaft and began to rise up to the surface.

The mine operated with day and night shifts. The miners were underground from 7 a.m. to 5 p.m. with one hour for lunch. On Sundays and national holidays, work was stopped in the mines except at the furnaces. Some workers were paid by the month, others by the day. For those underground, the contract system was in practice. The contract system motivated the men to give it their all. Their abilities were rewarded according to their production. The contract system was the most advantageous for both the company and the employee.

The Mine Shaft

Campbell

The Mine Shaft, 2004, 16 x 20 in.

The Blacksmith

The job of the blacksmith was much more than making, repairing, and fitting horseshoes. As a forger in iron, he was a master craftsman. The blacksmith held an important role in the community and mine operation. One of his tasks was to sharpen more than 1,000 drill bits every working day, by hand.

The wage for a blacksmith was $3.00 a day. His helpers received $1.25 to $2.00 a day. By comparison, the furnace foreman made $100 a month. A small house rented for $2.00 to $9.00 a month. Miners shopped in company stores where items often cost 25% more than in San Jose.

Each mine shaft area had its own shop, and there was one at the Hacienda Mine Works as well. To make a hot enough fire, a special coal was used. From the archives it was found that in 1865 James Butterworth ordered seven tons of coal, and in that same year the mine superintendent ordered an additional ten tons of blacksmith coal.

James B. Randol, the mine manager from 1870 to 1892, recognized the value of company-sponsored training, Randol established technical schools on the hill as well as at the Hacienda. Skills in cooking, sewing, carpentry, and blacksmithing were taught daily and were limited to two hours for five days a week. Prizes were offered to stimulate the youngsters to achieve in their training. In dressmaking, blacksmithing, carpentry, and mason work, class prizes of $10.00 were offered.

Items that blacksmith students learned besides shoeing horses were shaping iron, welding, tempering steel, drilling holes, and making bolts, staples, clevises, hooks, and the one item in constant demand, the candle holder.

> Many of the artifacts in the Almaden Quicksilver museum were from Connie Perham, who had the foresight to collect the rusted equipment and document the items realizing their historic value. Connie Perham even had a blacksmith shop in the museum she operated from 1949 to 1983.

The Blacksmith, 2003, 16 x 20 in.

Filling the Flasks

In this drawing, two men are filling flasks with quicksilver. A flask was 18 inches long and 8 inches in diameter. When filled, each flask held 76 pounds of mercury. When full, the flasks were marked with the initials of the Quicksilver Mining Co. A total of 200,000 flasks were produced from 1870 to 1883.

California annually produced about 75 percent of the nation's mercury. In 1970, due to sliding market price and fear of mercury contamination, almost every major quicksilver mine in California and Nevada shut down. The New Idria Mining & Chemical Co., the state's largest refinery of mercury, was still in operation. The New Almaden and Guadalupe mines were closed down in 1971. Other mines shut down were the Mt. Jackson Mine in Sonoma County, the Knoxville mine in Napa County, the Altuna mine in Trinity County, and the Buena Vista, the state's highest-grade mine, near Paso Robles.

Two smoke stacks were built on the top of the hill behind the Hacienda office as an early effort to clean up the hill. The fumes were piped to the stacks where they were released. Today, only one stack remains. The government warnings on mercury contamination of fish in Santa Clara Valley and the vaporous mercury in the air over the Mine Hill and part of the area around New Almaden have brought about the end of the mining industry in Santa Clara County.

Flasking Quicksilver, 2000, 16 x 20 in.

New Almaden's Hundred-Ton-A Day Smelter

In 1940, this hundred-ton rotary furnace was erected below Spanishtown's Big Rock to roast the ore obtained from open-cut mining. With power shovels and trucks, 1,000,000 tons of dumps and open cuts were dug out, which netted some 154,000 tons of ore running slightly over three pounds of mercury per ton of ore.

By May 19th 1971, due to the mercury contamination scares and sliding market price, almost every major quicksilver mine in California and Nevada had been shut down. California annually produced about 75 percent of the nation's mercury. The mine production dropped from a daily peak of 133 flasks in its heyday to only five flasks just before closing.

This drawing was made the day the mine was closed. Stockpiles of unrefined cinnabar ore lie in front of the smelter. Half a century later, there is still enough of the plant remaining to identify it.

The town of New Almaden has the only mercury mining museum in the United States. The original New Almaden Museum opened in 1949 and was operated by Constance Perham, a remarkable woman who displayed her collection of mercury memorabilia ranging from old mining tools to modern mercury switches. From this early museum, you begin to gain an appreciation of mercury. You are shown the distillation process and some of the many uses of mercury, from a thermometer to a thermos bottle to a fluorescent light.

Connie Perham believed her mother who used to say, "Nothing is ours; we are care-takers for the future." When she inherited the land and the adobe buildings from her parents, she dreamed of opening her own museum. Through her efforts, she convinced assorted groups of the historic significance of New Almaden, and in time the mine was declared a national historic landmark.

100 Ton Rotary Furnace, 2005, 16 x 20 in.

The Senator Mine

T he Senator Mine was located four miles northwest of Mine Hill. The Senator, or el Senador as the Mexican community knew it, was the most productive of the "Six Outside" mines on the New Almaden property. This mine was one of the three major mines, the others being the New Almaden and the Enriquita. This mine was sometimes referred to as the North Line Mine. The Senator was opened in 1863.

Jack Drew uncovered two unknown ore shoots and sank a vertical shaft 125 feet deep and encountered a mass of perfectly solid cinnabar three feet thick and the full height of the tunnel. This resulted in the recovery of more than 20,000 flasks of quicksilver.

The Senator's tunnel went straight into the hill for some 1,200 feet, dipping to the 1,300 foot level. This mine had 15 main levels. There were about 21,000 feet of tunnels in total length. It was 1,290 feet deep from the crest of the ridge to 600 feet below sea level.

Ore was found near the crest of the North slope in the early 1860's. But due to the remoteness of the mine to the Hacienda furnace plant, which was seven miles over the hills by horse and wagon, the work stopped. During the next 46 years it was mined off and on and yielded a small amount of ore. At the time of its closing in March 1926, there were still offices, cottages, and a boarding house beside the mine buildings. Maude, the mule that pulled the ore cars from deep in the mine, grazed on the hill above the tunnel.

Mercury was the accepted detonator for the explosives during World War I. In 1914, the price per flask went from $40.00 to $300.00. It stabilized at $100.00 in 1917. Today, the price of mercury is about $500.00 to $700.00 per flask.

The Senator Mine, 2005, 16 x 20 in.

The Almaden Station

The railroad in Almaden Valley began in 1886, when the South Pacific Coast railroad created a branch line from the gravel pit one mile South of Loveladys (today known as Campbell), heading out towards New Almaden. The line ended at a small depot on the banks of the Alamitos Creek.

Less than four months later, a rival line was created by the Southern Pacific Company. It was called the San Jose and Almaden railroad. The two competing railroad lines crossed one another and each had stations within a hundred yards of each other. The South Pacific Coast line ended south of Harry Road and east of the Alamitos Creek. The depot for the Southern Pacific line was west of the Alamitos Creek and north of McKean on what is now Cahen Drive.

The Southern Pacific Company ran a branch line, standard gauge, from San Jose to New Almaden, a distance of twelve miles. This was a daily freight and passenger train. The branch line service began operation November 16, 1886 and played an important part in serving passenger and freight service during the boom years of quicksilver mining. The depot was located about two miles from the settlement and passengers had to complete the journey by stagecoach.

Railroads running to Almaden existed for 48 years. Gone are the days when steam engines arrived at the station on the banks of the Alamitos Creek, where the stagecoach was waiting for you to complete your trip up the Alamitos Canyon to the Hacienda reduction works and the Casa Grande in New Almaden.

New Almaden Station, 2004, 16 x 20 in.

From San Jose to Hacienda

A daily stage coach left the Hacienda for San Jose and returned in the late afternoon. Workers, visitors, shopkeepers, and business people rode this long 12-mile dusty road to New Almaden. Fortunately there were stage stops every two miles: at Curtner, at Branham Lane, at Redmond Road, and at the predecessor of the Almaden Feed and Fuel, a popular local hangout, now closed. Two stage lines made the twelve-mile trip each way; travelers could reach the mines within four to five hours. If you journeyed by horse and buggy, it took about two hours. In the 1890's six miles an hour by the stage was considered average on a good day.

Teamsters who ran the stage were among the best-paid employees, often making as much as $100 per month.

Stage Coach   *Campbell*

Stage Coach, 2005, 16 x 20 in.

Spanishtown

Barron, Forbes Company brought workers in from Mexico to work the mine in 1850. An arroyo known as Deep Gulch extended from the base of Mine Hill to the community of Spanishtown. Today, there is very little to be seen of this picturesque settlement of scattered homes and white picket fences, vegetables and flower gardens that made up the Mexican camp. Many of the homes clung to the rocky hillside, accessible only by narrow footpaths. The daily life of the Spanish-speaking people soon transformed into a colorful and harmonious environment. The company owned and operated the facilities and rented the homes to the miners. Many of the inhabitants raised chickens, and had a cow, mule, or burro. The camp was also a home to many dogs.

During the long summer season, Deep Gulch maintained a warm temperature. In the late afternoon, an occasional breeze from the bay cooled the evenings enough for people to visit their neighbors or relax on their front porches. The sound of the guitar and children playing reflected a peaceful settlement. The people here enjoyed their way of life and the many traditional customs and religious functions. There was a bakery, tamale house, fruit store, barbershop, second-hand store, and shoemaker. They tended to make Spanishtown self-sufficient.

A Catholic church was located on a hill overlooking Deep Gulch. The church was built about 1885 by community contributions and company aid in money and supplies. There was a bell tower separate from the building, and on Sunday morning, the bell could be heard throughout Mine Hill. In the vicinity of the plaza there was a small schoolhouse where one teacher taught about twenty-five children in grades one to four. From the fourth grade on, children completed their schooling in Englishtown.

Spanishtown was burned several times due to the hot summers and dry redwood shanties. There was little the residents could do but gather their possessions and run for their lives. The settlement was built high on a hill and water was not close at hand.

Spanishtown, 2006, 16 x 20 in.

St. Anthony's Church at Spanishtown

The first St. Anthony's church was built in 1855. It overlooked Deep Gulch and Spanishtown. Spanishtown had several fires and twice the church was burned to the ground. The church in this drawing is the third church building to be built in Spanishtown. It was built in 1885, with community and mining company contributions. This building included stained glass windows, an organ, and a separate bell tower. Every Sunday morning the vibrant tone of the bell could be heard throughout the surrounding hills. Due to declining population, this church was abandoned in 1912.

St. Anthony's Church at the Hacienda was built in 1899 and is still in use today.

Señora Guadalupe Madera prayed for the safe return of her son, who fought in the Spanish-American War in the Philippines. Señora Madera, who ran the mine boarding house for many years, used her savings and solicited help and contributions from the miners and the Quicksilver Mining Company. This beautiful church was built when her son Antonio returned from the Philippines.

St. Anthony's Church, 2008, 16 x 20 in.

Mexican Miners

The first full-scale mining operation did not get underway until July of 1850. In the early days, Mexican laborers used strong leather packs called "zurons" to carry the ore out of the mine tunnels. The weight was largely supported by headbands that ran across the packer's forehead. The laborer would carry from 150 to 250 pounds of ore in this manner. The work by early miners was done by human muscle; there was no machinery. The workings below the main tunnel were likely to be hot and humid, and the laborers wore as little clothing as possible. Above the main tunnel, much of the ground was soft and broken. The tunnels required a virtual forest of timbers. The Mexican miners were not masters in the art of timbering, and many of the excavations collapsed. However, the Mexicans were masters in mauling a drill with short strokes in spaces smaller than a coffin.

Some of the best rock miners in the world came to New Almaden from Mexico. At one time 2,000 men, mostly Mexicans, were living on Mine Hill with their families. The work was hard and working conditions were poor at best. Wages were $1.75 a day. When gold was found in Alaska, many good men left the mine and went north to Alaska. It became difficult to find good men, even at $2.00 a day.

Much of the mining was done on contract. It was possible for a miner to make as much as $75.00 a week, although a third of this would be nearer to the average. No matter what a Mexican miner earned, he was often broke just before payday.

Mexican miners were known for their skills for finding rich cinnabar veins. Many small tunnels were dug and vast quantities of low-grade ore were uncovered. In 1874, the price of quicksilver reached an all-time high of $118.57 a flask. In 1879 the old Guadalupe mine produced 15,540 flasks, the largest output in a single year of any mine in California except New Almaden.

Mexican Miners, 2006, 16 x 20 in.

Cinnabar is the ore from which quicksilver is extracted. The Chinese used brilliant red cinnabar to paint their temples; some of the early American Indians used it to paint their bodies, until they became ill and feverish, then it was avoided as bad medicine. When the first samples of the ore were assayed at 35%, this proved to be far richer than the famous mine in Spain.

The Hanging Tree

New Almaden was not always the peaceful little settlement that it is today. During the mining days at New Almaden, justice was often dished out with a rope around the killer's neck. One memorable execution occurred in the late 1800s when a man who had raped or killed a girl was hanged from a tree. That tree is near the ruined settlement known as Spanishtown. This once-majestic oak was ideal for such happenings. One branch juts out for at least 25 feet, a dozen or so feet off the ground. And on the other side, just a bit higher, a branch shows signs of wear across the top.

After a hanging, it was the custom for passers-by to toss a small rock under the tree to express their distaste for the crime. The old tree still stands after its last execution, a lonely sentinel on the hill near what was once a settlement known as Spanishtown.

> The favorite Mexican holiday was Holy Week before Easter. Spanishtown miners would hang an effigy of the disciple Judas, filling it with fireworks and a live cat. As the fireworks were lit, the cat was released, symbolizing the release of Judas' soul.

The Hanging Tree, 2007, 16 x 20 in.

The Guadalupe Mine 1879

The heyday of the Guadalupe Mine to the west of Mine Hill was in the 1870s. Between 1875 and 1881 the mine produced 53,000 flasks, the largest output in a single year of any mine in California except the New Almaden. But the rich workings finally gave out under a creek that lavishly irrigated the mine tunnels. The Redington mine was full of gas, and the Sulphur Bank mine stood in a bank of boiling, sulfurous water that became hotter as the mine descended. Even with the handicaps, between 1875 and 1881 the Sulphur Bank mine produced 60,000 flasks, the Guadalupe produced 53,000 and the New Almaden produced 142,000. The Guadalupe's ore had bottomed out on the 900 foot level.

Mercury played an important role in the amalgamation system for mining gold and silver. By 1890 a new process for the reduction of gold and silver ore was materializing; cyanidation, which was later augmented by the floatation process. These new processes pushed aside the need for mercury. Despite this setback, American quicksilver mines flourished on a modest scale.

Early in the twentieth century, quicksilver was discovered in Texas, Oregon, and Nevada. California no longer held a monopoly. James Randol and the other Californians had dominated the mercury market, but by the time Randol retired, the aura of the California quicksilver mines had began to dim.

Guadalupe Mine, 2000, 16 x 20 in.

Delivering Firewood

One of the tasks for young Mexican boys was to deliver stove wood to the cottages in the mining settlement. During the fall season it was a common sight to see Mexican boys with their mules or burros, delivering stove wood from the nearby hills. These animals carried two large 300-pound bundles on their backs. The crude cinching of the load caused harsh abrasion on the hides of the mules.

The mining company owned several thousand acres of forest. They used about 600 cords of wood each month to fire their furnaces in the processing of mercury until they were able to obtain coal, and eventually oil.

Wood Deliveries, 2005, 16 x 20 in.

Englishtown Schoolhouse

An elementary school was established on the Mine Hill in Englishtown in 1864. The building was erected on a site overlooking the town center. This drawing depicts the school in its early years. For over forty years, it served the educational needs of the young population. As the years went by, fencing and landscaping were completed. Many of the miners had received little formal education while growing up and they were highly enthusiastic about seeing their children receiving an adequate education. The total education consisted of grades one through eight. For some of the graduates who had the interest and aptitude, J.B. Randol sponsored a technical program to further prepare the student who was about to become a worker. The boys were offered vocational training in carpentry, blacksmithing, and general mechanics. The girls were given classes in cooking and sewing.

The Hill School employed four teachers, one of whom was the principal. The school enrollment was at its greatest during the 1800s. In 1886, 253 students were in attendance. School teachers in the average mining community were the more rugged and adventuresome type, famous for their manner of strictness. It was not uncommon to display the ever conspicuous strap to impress on the students who was in charge. Adequate books and supplies were furnished to the students, who were responsible for loss or damage.

A one-room schoolhouse was located in Spanishtown to serve the Mexican children. In the greater percentage of the homes, only Spanish was spoken, which made the teacher's chores much more difficult. After fourth grade, the children went to Englishtown to complete the Upper Grade work. The average enrollment was about 35 and the teacher received $70 a month. By the turn of the century, the little schoolhouse was vacated for lack of students.

Englishtown School 1864, 2005, 16 x 20 in.

Life was not dull for the children of the miners. Young people were indoctrinated at an early age in assuming certain responsibilities. Boys took care of the wood supply and, in some cases, milked a cow, raised rabbits, or took care of the chickens. The girls in their early years became proficient in all areas of cooking, sewing, and general housework.

The company built the school and most of the homes for the miners. The houses were varied in size from four to eight rooms, and rental charge was from $2 to $9 a month. The houses were available only to employees and their families. There were a small number who built their own houses, and paid the ground fee of 50 cents a month. Many of the homes were enclosed with white picket fences and colorful gardens. In the early years people had to transport their own water or patronize a delivery service in which water was delivered in small barrels carried by burros.

Englishtown Church

In Englishtown stood the Methodist Episcopal Church, which faced a northern panorama of the Santa Clara Valley. The drawing pictured here is the last of the three structures that served the religious and social life of the Cornish community. The first church was built about 1871, but during the first winter a severe storm wrecked the building beyond repair. A second church was built in 1884, but after several years, fire razed it to the ground. The third and final church was erected at a cost of $3,400, which was financed by contributions from the community and the mining company.

For most people, the social activities were closely associated with the church. There were annual potluck picnics held under the spreading oak trees at the rear of the church. During the evening hours, the group assembled in the church basement for entertainment offered by individual members.

A Catholic Church was located on a hill overlooking Deep Gulch and the scattered homes of Spanishtown. The church was built about 1885 with community help and support from the mining company. The bell tower was separate from the main building and on Sunday morning the bell could be heard throughout the Cinnabar Hills.

Englishtown Church, 2005, 16 x 20 in.

The Garfield Shaft

The Garfield Shaft was started in 1881. When President Garfield was assassinated (September 1881), the name was changed to the Washington Shaft. When the Buena Vista pumps began operating in 1885, the Santa Isabel was connected with the Washington. The task of connecting the two shafts was done by a hand-picked crew of 12 miners who ran 700 feet of tunnel, including the incline between the 1,100 and the 1,400 foot level. The work was done in three months.

When this project was finished, the Washington Shaft was closed because a seepage of 75 gallons of water per minute developed in the shaft. The water had to be pumped out through the Buena Vista. The Washington Shaft was sunk to the 1,100 foot level, but below 850 feet the vein had not produced the way it was expected and further work was terminated in 1887.

The Garfield Shaft, 2000, 16 x 20 in.

The Bell Tower 1924

In 1874, the Hacienda experienced a fire that destroyed many of the miners' homes. Not long after, James Randol installed a system of fire hydrants and a bell tower with a hose cart. For many years this structure served for many occasions to alert the village and call the bucket brigade to action. By 1924, the bell tower was in need of much repair. Nearby, a fire station was added at the Hacienda, where the volunteer fire department would begin their journey to preventing the spread of the fire.

The Bell Tower 1924, 2008, 16 x 20 in.

The Good Times

Relaxation from the rigors of hard-rock mining was enjoyed in various ways by the folks in the mining community. The Spanishtown population had many more occasions for celebration than did their conservative neighbors, the Cornish miners in Englishtown. They both enjoyed hunting and fishing and the Helping Hand Club, where employees and their families could spend time leisurely.

The villages were entertained at various community functions by the colorful costumed brass band, which played a popular role in the life of this mining settlement. The Mountain Echo Band was organized on the hill in 1890, made up of members from Spanishtown and Englishtown. A baseball team, complete with a mascot, played visiting teams from surrounding townships. Both the Spanishtown and Englishtown communities enjoyed barbeques and dancing.

There were also two lodges, Cinnabar Lodge 199, Knights of Pythias, and General Gordon Lodge, No. 286, Sons of St. George. Most of the members of General Gordon were from the rugged shores of Cornwall. Church and lodge activity played an important part in this mining community of New Almaden. Payday, which the Mexicans called *Dia de Raya* (day of plenty), was always a big day. The employees of the mine received their wages at the end of each month. They received their pay in silver dollars.

> The spirit of New Almaden still prevails and is colorfully expressed with an annual parade held to commemorate the "Old Almaden Days."

Party Time 1890, 1999, 16 x 20 in.

Map of Almaden

This map was drawn in 1978 using an earlier map by Jimmie Schneider as a guide. This area today is known as New Almaden and the Almaden Quicksilver County Park, owned by the Santa Clara County Parks and Recreation Department.

Prior to 1863, the Berryessa claim, owned by the Barron, Forbes Company was to the right of the almost vertical line that runs through the middle of the map. To the left of the line the land was known as the Fossat claim and was owned by the Quicksilver Mining Company. When the U.S. Supreme Court decided that the claim boundaries were to be judged by true north instead of the magnetic north then drawn, the Barron, Forbes Company no longer had any mining rights, though they continued to own the Hacienda Settlement and the Mine Works to the right of the line. The Quicksilver Mining Company purchased the Barron, Forbes Company claim for $1,750,000 in 1863. The Quicksilver Mining Company then owned about 8,800 acres of land beginning at the confluence of the Calero Creek into Los Alamitos Creek and encompassing most of the map area.

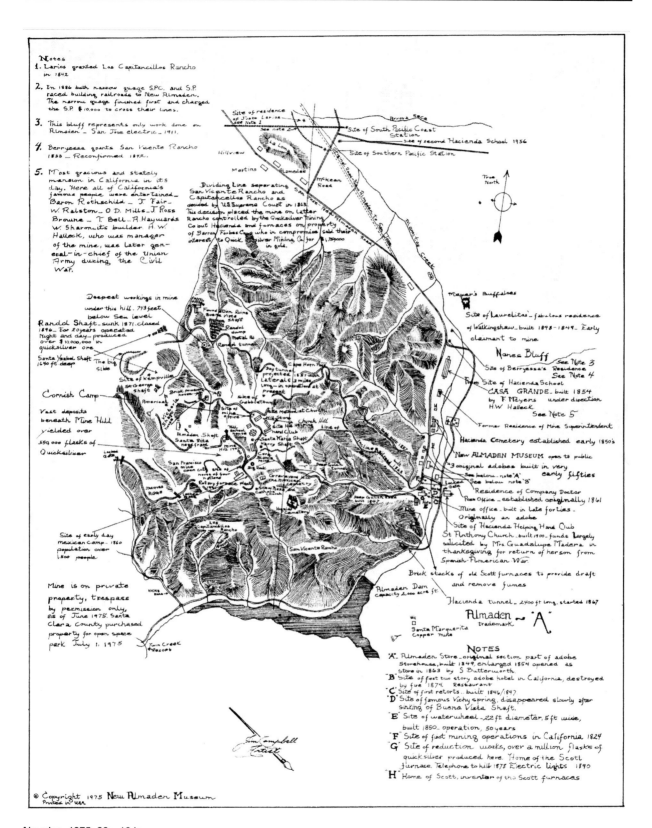

Almaden, 1975, 20 x 16 in.

Bibliography

Books listed here were valuable in researching information for this book. Readers may find the following books valuable companions. Some are available for sale at the New Almaden Quicksilver Mining Museum.

Allen, Rebecca and Mark Hylkema. *Life Along the Guadalupe River.* San Jose, CA: The Press, 2002.

Bailey, Edgar H. and Donald L. Everhart. *Geology and Quicksilver Deposits of the New Almaden District Santa Clara County California.* U.S. Government Printing Office, 1964.

Bradley, Walter W. *Quicksilver Resources of California.* California State Printing Office, 1918.

Browne, J. Ross. "Down in the Cinnabar Mines." *Harper's New Monthly Magazine,* Volume XXXV, 1865.

Christy, Samuel B. *Quicksilver Condensation at New Almaden,* California. Sherman and Company, Printers, 1885.

Demers, Donald O., ed. *Life in the Mines of New Almaden.* San Jose, CA: San Jose Historical Museum Association, 1978.

Foote, Mary Hallock. "A California Mining Camp." *Scribner's Monthly,* February 1878.

Johnson, Kenneth M. *The New Almaden Quicksilver Mine.* Georgetown, CA: The Talisman Press, 1963.

Lanyon, Milton and Laurence Bulmore. *Cinnabar Hills.* Los Gatos, CA: Village Printers, 1967.

McKinney, Gage. *A High and Holy Place.* Sunnyvale, CA: Pine Press, 1997.

Neilson, Rich. *The History of the Chinese at the New Almaden Quicksilver Mine: 1850 -1900.* Unpublished.

Peterson, Douglas and Linda Yamane. *The Ohlone People of Central California*. Santa Clara County Parks and Recreation Department.

Schneider, Jimmie. *Quicksilver*. San Jose, CA: Zella Schneider, 1992.

Vallejo, Mariano Guadalupe and Padre Francisco Palou. *Great Indians of California*, Santa Barbara, CA: Bellerophon Books, 1999.

Winn, S. E. and Robert Bulmore. *Views of New Almaden*. San Jose, CA: 1878.